FINANCIAL Committees

Thomas A. McLaughlin

Book Three of the BoardSource Committee Series

Formerly the National Center for Nonprofit Boards

Library of Congress Cataloging-in-Publication Data

McLaughlin, Thomas A.
Financial committees / by Thomas A. McLaughlin.
p. cm. — (BoardSource committee series ; 3)
ISBN 1-58686-070-4 (pbk.)
1. Nonprofit organizations—Finance. 2. Management committees.
I. Title. II. Series.
HG4027.65.M347 2004
658.15'9—dc22
2003016227

First printing, November 2003.
ISBN 1-58686-070-4

Published by BoardSource
1828 L Street, NW, Suite 900
Washington, DC 20036

Formerly the National Center for Nonprofit Boards

BoardSource, formerly the National Center for Nonprofit Boards, is the premier resource for practical information, tools and best practices, training, and leadership development for board members of nonprofit organizations worldwide. Through our highly acclaimed programs and services, BoardSource enables organizations to fulfill their missions by helping build strong and effective nonprofit boards.

BoardSource provides assistance and resources to nonprofit leaders through workshops, training, and our extensive Web site, www.boardsource.org. A team of BoardSource governance consultants works directly with nonprofit leaders to design specialized solutions to meet organizations' needs and assists nongovernmental organizations around the world through partnerships and capacity building. As the world's largest, most comprehensive publisher of materials on nonprofit governance, BoardSource offers a wide selection of books, videotapes, and CDs. BoardSource also hosts the National Leadership Forum, bringing together approximately 800 governance experts, board members, and chief executives of nonprofit organizations from around the world.

Created out of the nonprofit sector's critical need for governance guidance and expertise, BoardSource is a 501(c)(3) nonprofit organization that has provided practical solutions to nonprofit organizations of all sizes in diverse communities. In 2001, BoardSource changed its name from the National Center for Nonprofit Boards to better reflect its mission. Today, BoardSource has more than 15,000 members and has served more than 75,000 nonprofit leaders.

For more information, please visit our Web site at www.boardsource.org, e-mail us at mail@boardsource.org, or call us at 800-883-6262.

Have You Used These BoardSource Resources?

Videos

Meeting the Challenge: An Orientation to Nonprofit Board Service

Speaking of Money: A Guide to Fund-Raising for Nonprofit Board Members

Building a Successful Team: A Guide to Nonprofit Board Development

Books

The Board Chair Handbook

Managing Conflicts of Interest: Practical Guidelines for Nonprofit Boards

Checks and Balances: The Board Member's Guide to Nonprofit Financial Audits

The Board-Savvy CEO: How To Build a Strong, Positive Relationship with Your Board

Presenting: Board Orientation

Presenting: Nonprofit Financials

The Board Meeting Rescue Kit: 20 Ideas for Jumpstarting Your Board Meetings

The Board Building Cycle: Nine Steps to Finding, Recruiting, and Engaging Nonprofit Board Members

The Policy Sampler: A Resource for Nonprofit Boards

To Go Forward, Retreat! The Board Retreat Handbook

Nonprofit Board Answer Book: Practical Guide for Board Members and Chief Executives

Nonprofit Board Answer Book II: Beyond the Basics

The Legal Obligations of Nonprofit Boards

Self-Assessment for Nonprofit Governing Boards

Assessment of the Chief Executive

Fearless Fundraising

The Nonprofit Board's Guide to Bylaws

Creating and Using Investment Policies

Transforming Board Structure: New Possibilities for Committees and Task Forces

The Governance Series

1. *Ten Basic Responsibilities of Nonprofit Boards*
2. *Financial Responsibilities of Nonprofit Boards*
3. *Structures and Practices of Nonprofit Boards*
4. *Fundraising Responsibilities of Nonprofit Boards*
5. *Legal Responsibilities of Nonprofit Boards*
6. *The Nonprofit Board's Role in Setting and Advancing the Mission*
7. *The Nonprofit Board's Role in Planning and Evaluation*
8. *How To Help Your Board Govern More and Manage Less*
9. *Leadership Roles in Nonprofit Governance*

For an up-to-date list of publications and information about current prices, membership, and other services, please call BoardSource at 800-883-6262 or visit our Web site at www.boardsource.org.

Contents

Preface

The BoardSource Committee Series is intended to provide board members and chief executives with a practical approach to determining an appropriate committee structure and details on the responsibilities of each committee. The following preface will convey the philosophy of the series as a whole, using ideas from the first book in the series, Transforming Board Structure: Strategies for Committees and Task Forces, *and general information on how to handle committee operations.*

It is virtually impossible to define a committee structure that can or should be adopted by every nonprofit board. The material below can be used as a set of guidelines as your board searches for the best way to manage its own operations.

First and foremost, it is important to understand the difference between the full board, committees, and task forces in context of one another. The *board* has a fiduciary duty for the organization and is legally liable for its activities. It is responsible for articulating the direction for the organization and overseeing that the directives are implemented effectively and in an ethical manner. To manage these objectives, the board naturally must structure itself to accomplish its work in the most efficient manner possible.

Committees, or for the purpose of this introductory discussion, *standing committees*, are groups comprised of board members and outsiders that ensure consistency and regularity in key board practices. They are groups that are always necessary in helping the full board carry out its work. Committees (with the executive committee as a common exception) normally do not make organizational decisions; therefore, their members do not carry liability, as do members of the full board.

Task forces, similar in purpose to committees, are usually created in order to carry out a specific objective within a certain amount of time. They are typically established on an as-needed basis, allowing greater flexibility in the work of the board and its individual members. With the help of task forces, immediate needs of the board can be handled more quickly — without having to reconstruct the other committees and their ongoing work plans.

Committees and task forces generally do the majority of the board's work between meetings, allowing the full board to keep its attention on important decisions and on the big picture of the organization's success in fulfilling its mission. They give individual board members an opportunity to contribute to the work of the board in ways they would not be able to in regular meetings. These work groups enable the full board to benefit from the special skills and expertise of its members in a concrete manner.

How Committees Are Formed

To provide all the flexibility possible for your committee structure, avoid listing the job descriptions for your committees and task forces in the bylaws. A simple statement indicating that the board may form committees and other work groups as needed is sufficient. An exception to this approach, however, is the executive committee. If your board finds it necessary to form an executive committee, its authority must be detailed in your legal document. (Please refer to *Transforming Board Structure* or *Executive Committee* for more information.)

Your bylaws should also clarify who has the power to form committees. The full board should discuss and agree on the need for a specific committee or task force. Naturally, the board should also make the initial purpose of each standing committee or task force as explicit as possible to avoid any situations where the committee might establish its own charge (or description of purpose). Responsibilities of each group may shift as circumstances change, so it is important to remain flexible in each group's charge. Usually the board chair chooses each committee chair and, in collaboration, they put together the rest of the group. Some boards require the chair's appointments to be approved by the board.

It is important to clarify the distinction between *board committees* and *organizational committees* in order to avoid any misunderstanding. Board committees report to the board and help carry out its mandate. Organizational committees, on the other hand, report to staff members and help with operational issues. They may serve as advisors to the staff and assist with issues that are staff members' responsibilities. In organizations with a small paid staff, organizational committees sometimes serve as volunteer staff to carry out the organization's work.

There is no reason for the board to duplicate staff work and form structures that collide with staff's duties. For example, if you have marketing staff, it is difficult to justify a board marketing committee. If your board includes marketing experts, there is nothing to prevent staff from asking for advice from knowledgeable board member(s) — who should be happy to oblige. If there is no staff dedicated to organizational marketing efforts, your board may consider forming a task force to look at relevant issues affecting the organization in this area. It is also possible to form an organizational committee that is more operational and composed of staff members, board specialists, and probably outsider experts.

Job Descriptions, Membership, and Size

As mentioned above, each committee or task force should have a written charter explaining its role, responsibilities, and accountability. Although the full board is responsible for agreeing on the objectives for each work group, the committee chair is responsible for leading the group in following its charter and staying focused. The committee chair communicates with the board, ensuring that appropriate reporting takes place.

It is a good idea to include varying perspectives among committee members to ensure that all aspects of an issue or task receive adequate consideration. By rotating board members in and out of different committees, the board provides possibilities for individual development. It is probably not wise, however, for an individual board member to serve on more than two committees at a time because of possible burnout. Sometimes board members who have a particular interest in learning or contributing to a specific subject or cause will request or volunteer to be on a specific committee. Additionally, not all committees are comprised solely of board members. Community leaders who can share a particular area of expertise can add to the quality of discussion. Work groups are also a great way for someone who is interested in being a board member to begin involvement with an organization. Organizational committees typically draw members from the community who can add innovation and proficiency in a specific subject. There are few committees, however, that are usually comprised of only board members (e.g., the executive committee).

When deciding on the optimal committee size, once again, no specific rule exists. It strongly depends on the purpose of the committee, scope of the task, and the size of the full board. A committee should always be small enough to keep all members thoroughly involved. Group dynamics can determine effective working relationships and consequently influence the size of the group.

Committee-Staff Relationships

Some board committees or task forces benefit from direct staff support. The chief executive can assign a staff person to relevant committees to help with background information, relate the context of the committee work to operational work, or to provide administrative support. Work groups should be careful not to inundate the staff member with unreasonable requests; after all, he or she usually has other responsibilities in addition to committee support.

Meeting Schedule, Minutes, and Reports

Determining a meeting schedule for committees or task forces should be done on an as-needed basis — there is no particular prescription for the timing and minimum or maximum meetings per year. Each group knows what is expected and must be able to determine the necessary measures to accomplish the task. With committees that have members in various areas of the country or abroad, it is possible to communicate over the telephone or electronically, as long as the desired work is getting done properly. (State laws may regulate board meetings but not committee meetings.) One frequently *ineffective* way to manage most committee meetings, however, is to schedule them in conjunction with the full board meeting in an attempt to take advantage of all members gathering in the same place at the same time. This causes repetitious conversation and agenda items and, ultimately, may be waste of time.

Each group also has the freedom to determine how to keep track of what happens in committee meetings. Work groups may or may not find it necessary to keep minutes, but most likely want to take some notes for purposes of reporting to the board or to keep track of particularly detailed information. For example, a development committee drafting action plans for the coming fiscal year will need to document decisions carefully.

It is advisable to circulate committee reports as part of the board consent agenda in the board package. This allows board members to familiarize themselves with the contents before the meeting and helps to eliminate the tradition of spending meeting time listening to committee reports. Major issues needing board debate should be placed on the main agenda.

Assessing the Need for Committees or Task Forces

In coming up with the most advantageous committee structure for your board, make sure that you continuously reassess the need for each work group. Unnecessary committees simply waste people's valuable time, misuse members' contributions and commitment, and provide no added value to the board. Some boards rely on a *zero-based committee structure*, disbanding all non-standing committees and task forces at the end of the year and reevaluating their necessity for the future — they start with a clean slate. It may still happen that a committee of the previous year gets reinstated but it may have a new composition of members or it may have a slightly changed charter. Whatever method your board uses to justify its internal structure, make sure that, ultimately, you have only committees and task forces that your organization needs and that they have all the resources necessary to function efficiently.

Introducing the Series

As we discussed above, there is no single right answer on how to structure a board or indicate how committees or task forces meet their expectations. Structures should never remain static and all boards should keep an open mind when experimenting with different options. Constant evaluation and flexibility are necessary during the search for optimal results. The best way to keep a committee structure simple is to limit the number of standing committees to what is absolutely essential, and to supplement these committees with less permanent structures.

With the Committee Series, BoardSource is providing additional information and guidance to help your board determine its structural options. The initial series consists of six books. The first book, *Transforming Board Structure*, sets the stage for committees in general. The next five books each cover the duties of common committees that many boards find necessary.

- *Transforming Board Structure* — introducing committee and task force structure
- *Governance Committee* (Book One) — relating to recruitment and education of board members
- *Executive Committee* (Book Two) — addressing how to use executive committees properly
- *Financial Committees* (Book Three) — defining the core duties of the finance, audit, and investment committees
- *Development Committee* (Book Four) — helping to involve your full board in fundraising
- *Advisory Councils* (Book Five) — describing the numerous roles that advisory groups or councils can play to help your nonprofit function more efficiently

Introduction

If you were to ask most members of a nonprofit's board of directors what they want their financial committees to accomplish, they would likely say: "To take over this area that we don't understand and don't want to spend time on, and make sure that we stay out of trouble." Clearly, participating in the work of financial committees does not rank high on the agenda of many board members.

Giving proper and focused attention to the responsibilities of your organization's financial committees can be very complicated and presumes a reasonable amount of specialized knowledge. The challenge with respect to effective governance, however, is that to simply transfer the responsibility of overseeing the finances of an organization to a smaller group of people runs the risk that this group may not be fully aware of how much time and expertise is required. In certain circumstances, particularly in troublesome economic times where there is little margin for error, this could prove to be a prescription for disaster. Thus, remaining willfully ignorant about what your board's financial committees are doing is simply not an option. The full board always remains the responsible and liable body of the organization and cannot delegate this duty to anyone else.

So, there is really no way around it. Board members, regardless of their predisposition, have to answer the essential questions: What *should* the various financial committees do? What are their main duties and what are their discretionary duties? When can one leading finance committee carry on all the duties and when is it necessary to delegate the tasks to separate and distinct subgroups?

Simply put, the principal finance committee that is part of every board oversees the financial planning and management of the organization by ensuring that all fiscal aspects of operations are in order. While there is no official list of mandatory activities, most advisors tend to agree about what a nonprofit should expect from its finance committee. For the purposes of this book, we will call these the *core duties*.

Non–core duties can be defined as responsibilities that the finance committee must perform in the absence of other committees dealing with financial issues, most notably a dedicated audit committee, which is specifically charged to oversee the independence of the organization's audit functions and its compliance with legal and ethical standards. Non–core duties can also include those responsibilities addressing investment decisions when there is no separate committee devoted to this function.

This book will first address the core and non–core duties separately as part of distinct committees or task forces. (Please see the chart in Appendix I for a short outline of all financial duties.) It will then discuss the numerous challenges that appear when a board is trying to handle all the financial issues with one core finance committee that has all the non–core tasks attached to it. Our purpose in presenting the material this way is to allow board members of all types of organizations to outline the structural elements for addressing financial duties in a manner that is most feasible for their particular nonprofit. The text will also elaborate on the subject of independence for board members and auditors.

By providing a basic overview of the duties of financial committees, it is intended that all members of the board, particularly those who are least knowledgeable about financial matters, will feel better guided to step into their fiduciary role. This material will not go into detail about overall financial responsibilities of board members or how to read financial statements (these are covered by other BoardSource publications; please see the Suggested Resources) but it focuses on the role of the financial committees as tools to help the board do its job more efficiently.

1 How To Determine the Configuration of Your Financial Committees

There are a great many possible combinations of structuring board committees to handle financial tasks. Common financial work groups often include finance committees, audit committees, investment committees, fundraising committees, and executive committees, with a possibility of others. Task forces can also be created to provide flexibility and efficiency for handling the various demands in the financial context of an organization. The particular configuration your board chooses will be determined by a variety of different factors.

Financial work groups are more demanding than all other board committees in terms of skills and expertise. This book is organized to help you decide what configuration to use in order to carry out both core and non–core financial oversight. For the very small organizations and the very large, the dividing lines will be clear. Small organizations will probably have to cover both core and non–core duties with a single finance committee. Larger organizations, on the other hand, will usually have more people and more resources to support additional committees responsible for further duties. The test to determine when your organization needs additional committees is mostly experiential — you will know it's time to have multiple committees when the task grows too big for a single financial committee to complete in an effective manner.

Many different factors may prompt a board to form multiple committees. The following examples address circumstances that influence the board's final choice.

The Right Reasons To Have Multiple Committees

Scope

As a nonprofit grows and its revenues increase, the scope of its financial activity changes. More revenue means not only that there will be more resources available to the organization, but also additional demands placed upon it. Increased revenue and resources may also require the board to diversify its oversight functions and share the responsibilities with different work groups. Creating separate finance-related committees may achieve these tasks in the most efficient way.

Nature of Financial Management Challenge

Even more than sheer scope, multiple or sophisticated revenue sources create considerable financial complexity. The interplay between different sources of funding also imposes added complexity, as the nonprofit has to find its way through complicated and sometimes conflicting requirements.

Moreover, when an organization receives federal funding, it is often driven to the next level of sophistication. A few hundred thousand dollars of federal funds, for example, is enough to trigger an audit that must be done according to specialized audit regulations issued by the federal Office of Management and Budget ("OMB A-133 audits"). Overseeing this compliance may require a dedicated committee or work group.

The presence of an endowment can also increase the board's financial responsibilities, since it assumes additional fiduciary duties in safeguarding and nurturing those funds. Even if the endowment is held in the form of stocks managed by financial professionals, the board still has the responsibility to oversee that relationship. A substantial endowment often requires a dedicated committee to oversee it separately from the traditional finance or audit committees.

Degree of Regulatory Oversight

Many board members of organizations receiving governmental funds often initially underestimate the degree of administrative oversight required to operate in a heavily regulated environment. In fact, governmental funders set regulations only on the use of the funds they specifically provide, not for the nonprofit as a whole. This is a subtle but very important distinction.

Most routine governmental oversight of nonprofits is by units of government agencies acting in their role as funders, not as pure regulators. In doing so, they are largely looking after the way their own funds are employed by the organization and protecting their own economic interests, not whether the organization is acting on behalf of the public at large. This is critical for board members to understand. It means that they must not rely on the government to supply most of the meaningful oversight but are responsible for doing it themselves.

Further, most of the general oversight is administrative anyway. Regulatory actions are usually taken in response to some sign of trouble or improper use of funds, as opposed to being the result of careful, proactive analysis. Such proactive analysis typically falls under the domain of dedicated board committees or task forces.

As public policy, this restrained governmental role is sensible. It limits the government's involvement in the general internal affairs of the organization. Nonprofits are designed to be accountable to the community.

In terms of both ethical behavior and statutory regulation, they are held to a high standard. It is thus reasonable to concentrate limited governmental enforcement resources in other areas where such presumed natural constraints predisposed to the public interest don't exist. But this also means that there is extra pressure on the board of directors voluntarily to ensure that their organization is in full compliance with its public obligations. Just responding to the pressure of civic expectation often requires multiple committees.

...And the Wrong Reasons for Multiple Committees

On occasion, a nonprofit board will feel the need to create a substantial system of financial oversight because it distrusts the staff's capabilities. This is *not* a good reason to establish additional financial committees. Rather, this is the time to examine the organization's fundamental processes. Install good people and good systems and this perceived need for excess supervision will disappear.

Some boards function according to old-fashioned and outdated governance principles. They create complicated committee structures without assessing a need for them. Why would a board have an investment committee if its small operational reserves are best kept in a local bank account?

Another reason why some boards create numerous committees has less to do with financial oversight, but involves installing systems that are expected to encourage others to join the board. High prestige figures in the community often seek to occupy high profile positions. Multiple finance committees would afford an opportunity to serve these needs of potential board members. However, there are numerous other ways to create opportunities for board members to shine rather than by creating an infrastructure that complicates and encumbers normal board processes.

How Do the Financial Committees Relate to Other Financial Bodies within the Organization?

The full board has the ultimate responsibility and fiduciary obligation to the organization, but it can delegate various *tasks* to the committees. Committee members do not have individual liability, as they make recommendations rather than binding organizational decisions.

The treasurer of the board is often closely affiliated with the finance committee and usually serves as its chair. This makes sense, as the treasurer supposedly has the needed financial acumen and, overall as a board officer, is closely involved in leading the board in financial thinking. A highly regarded treasurer also has the skill of making complicated fiscal issues more understandable and palatable for the rest of the board members.

The members of financial committees are only part of the entities or groups of individuals who are closely involved in the organization's fiscal matters. So that nobody steps on anyone else's toes or misunderstands his or her level of authority, it may be helpful to outline the relationships between these different actors. Job descriptions always serve their purpose, as defining authorities and needed boundaries are strongly advised.

Finance committee members collaborate closely with senior financial staff, notably the chief financial officer and, of course, the chief executive. The chief financial officer oversees the staff activities that relate to financial issues, acts as the key person to move the annual budget into the committee's hands, and ensures that accurate and timely financial statements reach the full board regularly. The finance committee can serve as the main support for the chief financial officer during planning and budget preparation but it is important to draw a line between getting too involved and serving as useful advisors. Naturally, if there is no position for a chief financial officer, the chief executive plays that role.

Audit committee members have an important role of communicating the need for high morals and ethical behavior for every board member, and ensuring that the staff is following similar principles. The chief executive and the chief financial officer must understand the committee's objectives clearly.

The investment committee mainly deals with the outside investment manager and reports to the full board. Members rarely need to interact directly with staff.

2 The Finance Committee

A board that is able to separate its various financial tasks among individual committees or task forces is in a better position to focus on key duties for each. Segregation of duties allows the board to benefit from specific skills that exist on the board. Equally, it provides for added accountability when oversight for financial management and independent audit are fully detached.

Your finance committee should be organized around a handful of fundamental chores. The committee should concentrate on these core duties and let the other fiscal committees handle the rest of the financial issues on the board's agenda.

The Core Functions of the Finance Committee

- Oversees organizational financial planning
- Monitors that adequate funds are available for the plan
- Safeguards organizational assets
- Drafts organizational fiscal policies
- Anticipates financial problems
- Ensures that the board receives accurate and complete information
- Helps the rest of the board understand financial statements and the general financial situation of the organization
- Makes sure that federal, state, and local reporting takes place
- Sustains the committee itself

Oversee Financial Planning

During the strategic planning process it is essential for all financial opportunities and constraints to be calculated into the plan. The finance committee has a key role in the planning by participating in the expert analysis of the external and internal environment that determines the future course for the organization. The ultimate strategic plan drives all other planning inside the organization — within a realistic financial framework.

As board representatives, the finance committee members work closely with the senior financial staff to ensure that the budget process is efficiently carried out. In carrying out this core duty, a board of directors will find that there is a fine line between exercising oversight on the one hand and actually executing action on the other. This is one of the duties where there is likely to be a wide variation in how boards and staff work together. Some groups prefer to have the finance committee operate with a budget review-and-approve approach, while others may want to be more involved in actually developing the budget. This decision is most strongly influenced by the organization's size, number of financial staff members, and sophistication of the financial management tasks. The smaller the nonprofit, the more likely that board members will be involved in the development of the budget and the monitoring systems.

Even if drafting the budget is generally a staff function, committee members can provide additional — and often welcome — feedback to staff on the big picture issues that relate to the strategic plan. Collaboration with financial staff during the budgeting process eliminates misunderstandings and wrong assumptions about the board's future directives. The board ultimately must approve the budget — so why not initially ensure that the key elements are included and that previously made decisions get properly interpreted in the figures?

Once again, we underscore the importance of reliable financial information. The following list provides some indicators of a superior budget system.

- There is a defined yearly cycle of budget development and monitoring.
- The budgeting process is explicitly linked to the overall strategic plan.
- Budget development includes program managers' ideas.
- Managers distinguish between operating budgets and budgets for capital investments (such as real estate, vehicles, computers, etc.).
- All managers receive regular budget reports on their areas of responsibility.
- The finance committee has its own set of regular budget reports.
- Managers are held accountable for their budget performance.

Don't Get Stuck on Your Budget

It seems that managers' most common complaint about board members in budget matters goes something like this: *"They won't let us change it!"* Some boards want the organization to craft a budget by the beginning of the year and then stick with it until the end, without any changes. Budgets are planning tools, not handcuffs. Don't be afraid to make adjustments when circumstances demand it, but make every effort to put together a budget that is well researched and relies on relevant data. If a major grant comes through or fails to materialize, or other extraordinary incidents change the course for the organization, naturally your guidelines must reflect the changes or else they become irrelevant. Failing to follow the original guidance in the budget is not a valid reason to make adjustments to the figures. In that case, go back to the starting line, analyze what you did wrong, and then correct your actions.

Monitor That Adequate Funds Are Available for Financial Management Tasks

Without assurance that the planned budgeted activities are covered by adequate available funding, no financial planning is worth the initial effort. Using a bird's eye view on the evolution of all activities — fundraising, the rest of the revenues, and all accrued expenses included — gives the committee the ability to keep track of the bottom line as it monitors the financial statements it receives from the staff on a regular basis. The committee's duty is to spot the red flags and explain the variances to the rest of the board — after the staff has justified any discrepancies.

Ensure That Assets Are Protected

The fiduciary duty of nonprofit boards is grounded in a bedrock of legal theories of accountability. Nonprofit boards of directors truly are given responsibility for a quasi-public entity, and thus their corresponding duty is to make sure they do nothing to damage it. This is one of the reasons why boards of directors usually must approve major transactions, such as the purchase or sale of buildings and other major assets, lest the financial viability of the organization be jeopardized.

This fiduciary responsibility prompts specific related duties that often fall to the finance committee. One of the most common is to oversee investing of the reserves or the endowment (although sometimes that is done by a separate committee, the executive committee, or even by the full board). Maintaining oversight to ensure that a system of internal control is in place is another way that finance committees can protect a nonprofit's assets if the audit committee does not specifically oversee this important aspect of the organization's finances.

Paradoxically, however, some finance committees can be overzealous in the opposite direction, becoming overly concerned with avoiding financial risk to the point of inaction, and unwilling to consider anything remotely resembling innovation. A predictably unfortunate situation is when a too-protective finance committee causes a nonprofit to build up large reserves that might better be used to support programming.

By drafting appropriate financial policies, the committee acts as a protector of the organization's assets. Proactive protection eliminates situations where a disaster may happen due to unavailable guidelines. Here again, the committee must focus on "big" issues that impact major financial decisions; the committee must not get involved in staff-related processes that are governed by employment policies and procedure manuals.

Draft Organizational Fiscal Policies

Fiscal policies serve as guidelines — and protection — for board and staff as they address all the numerous complicated and routine questions relating to the financial management and oversight that affect the organization. These policies act as reference tools for appropriate action, ethical decision making, and for dealing with potential or actual conflicts. Some of these policies can paraphrase a legal or accounting regulation, explain a procedure, clarify a principle, or express a desired goal. When properly used, they help diminish embarrassing or potentially harmful situations, improper behavior, and ineffective decision making.

The challenge for the committee is to realize where the line is drawn between everyday procedures and overall organizational policies. The committee has no need to get involved in defining processes for staff. It should let the staff determine its methods for tasks such as handling check requests, opening the mail, endorsing the checks, selecting which credit cards to be accepted, or processing refunds. The committee will draft policies for board approval that deal with acceptable reserves for the organization, the board's involvement in signing major purchases or financial commitments, or appropriate use of board-designated funds.

Anticipate Financial Problems

Being an educated clairvoyant is one of the most valued assets of a competent finance committee. Committee members with a thorough understanding of and interest in general financial issues that frame the environment within which the organization functions are in an advantageous position to guide the board's fiscal decision making. No organization functions in a vacuum. World economics, market fluctuations, political powers shaping the country's fiscal policies, regional issues affecting the financial viability of the communities, changing industry standards, or local demographic transformations can affect the money flow within an individual nonprofit.

An ability to draw the links between the external environment and its potential influence on the organization is just as important as assessing internal structures and processes. The committee must be tuned to factors that provide a breeding ground for financial mismanagement or fraud. Here again, being farsighted and proactive is the best approach in avoiding financial disasters.

Oversee Financial Record Keeping

Any financial department tends to produce voluminous information. Finance committees have multiple responsibilities in this regard, but the first step is making sure that the information exists. Secondarily, it is important that this information remains accurate, complete, and useable.

Board members on a finance committee are at a slight disadvantage in their attempt to oversee the financial record keeping. They never have a chance to get inside the record-keeping systems or to dig around to see how well these systems work. Therefore, they have to find other ways of assessing the information they are presented.

Committee members charged with overseeing financial data have two mandates with respect to the information: What does it mean? How reliable is it? This book focuses mainly on the reliability of the information rather than the implications of its meaning (for guidance in how board members can interpret financial information, see Suggested Resources on page 38).

Fortunately, board members have many ways of assessing the reliability of the information their organization's financial staff produces. Nothing is more important than their communication with the agency's auditor. This information pathway is so essential that we will spend all of Chapter 3 focusing on it. Here are some other ways to judge the information you receive.

Does It Exist?

The simple existence of financial reports is perhaps the single key indicator of the adequacy of your record-keeping system. The fact that an organization can produce financial information *at all* is a threshold for oversight of the record-keeping system. When the staff seems to consistently have an excuse for the unavailability of financial data — the computer system went down, someone got sick, the bank was running late transmitting the records — it is a warning sign that the organization has not yet crossed this threshold.

Is It Timely?

Are the financial reports produced regularly? At the end of every month the staff must close the books and records. Shortly afterward, it should be prepared to produce reports for that month. Except in the very smallest of nonprofits, complete records should be available for any given month within no more than about 15 calendar days or fewer after the month ends. Moreover, with today's financial accounting software, accountants should be able to produce accurate records at practically any time. Remember — the longer you wait for financial information, the staler it becomes.

Is It Helpful?

Record keeping amounts to little if its output is not useful. Of course, *useful* has different meanings for different groups, but the key is that the numbers make sense to you as board members. Most accounting packages have standard reporting templates built into the program, but that does not mean that the output is useful or even understandable to a nontechnical audience. It may be worthwhile to create a set of customized reports for your organization that help monitor your particular set of indicators. There are no absolute standards for what a good system of financial reports looks like (it depends on your explicit needs), though there are many traditional models.

If the board is not receiving what it needs, the finance committee must step in and clarify the specific reports desired and which data must be included in what format.

Does It Hold Up Over Time?

Does the financial information you obtain seem to hold up over time without after-the-fact adjustments? In other words, are you reasonably sure that the numbers will not change and have to be restated? If so, you can probably assume that you are receiving accurate information being produced by a high-quality system. The annual financial audit is a good checkpoint here. A useful guide: Is the information in the last month's financial reports different from that in the yearly audit? If so, by how much? The greater the discrepancy, the more likely it is that you have been receiving erroneous information all year, and that the auditors found it necessary to make substantial corrections.

Does It Pass the "Smell" Test?

Financial matters for many people are understandably shrouded in mystery. The knowledge required to understand and analyze their implications is specialized and technical. It is natural, given the complexity that many board members feel when they are working out of their depth in examining a balance sheet or monthly income statement. No one wants to go into an area where he or she fears being revealed as ignorant or incapable. Yet, some of the best insights into financial matters can come from old-fashioned, common sense. If you are given financial information that does not seem to add up, question it! Even if the apparent discrepancy turns out to be completely innocuous, you have sent the important message that you are paying attention.

Help the Full Board Understand the Organization's Financial Health

One of the most valuable roles a finance committee can play is to be the intermediary between the financial aspects of a nonprofit corporation and the rest of the board of directors. Recall that we began this document with the frank acknowledgment that finance committee members are usually asked to take responsibility for an area that the rest of their board colleagues feel uncomfortable overseeing. At the same time, the full board needs understandable financial information in order to carry out its duties properly. Thus, it is the finance committee's responsibility to fill this gap by serving as a kind of communication channel to the rest of the board, translating financial data into meaningful terms that can be understood.

Like most technical fields, financial management has its share of jargon that can be off-putting for those unfamiliar with it. The job of the finance committee is not unlike that of a translator. One of the most effective things the committee can do is to position itself as a bridge between the financial staff, financial advisors, and the full board.

The translatorlike role of the finance committee is largely a metaphor, of course, but there are some concrete things that the committee can do to make the information more salient and comprehensible to untutored board members.

- Speak to the board about financial matters in plain English with as little technical jargon as possible, and insist that the staff and outside advisors do the same.
- Be willing to answer any questions, no matter how seemingly silly or irrelevant.
- Use words and language, including short notes or inserts into financial material, to support whatever message the numbers are expected to convey.
- Use graphics instead of or in addition to numbers or words. Most adults learn about unfamiliar subjects more quickly through visual means.
- Talk about the implications of a financial report; do not just describe its contents.
- Explicitly link the financial health of the organization with its goals and strategy. Explain why finances will or will not allow the organization to accomplish what it has set out to do.

Make Sure All Legal Reporting Requirements Are Met

The finance committee is often in the best position to help the board ensure that all federal, state, and local reporting takes place. If your board has a separate audit committee, this group, however, usually assumes that duty. Ultimately, it does not matter who takes the responsibility, as long as you avoid waiting until the government officials, or even your auditor, bring any negligence or misjudgment to your attention. (See Chapter 3 for more information.)

Sustain the Finance Committee Itself

Finally, the finance committee has to sustain its own membership. It cannot be denied that the demand for qualified and financially savvy board members is getting tougher. Even for-profit companies, now legally required to have at least one financial expert on their audit committee, are tapping into the available pool of candidates. Nonprofit boards must take recruitment seriously and reserve the necessary time for the hunt and subsequent training. If your new (or old) board members do not have the needed acumen, there are numerous training tools to start correcting this situation.

As is true with other board members, finance committee members should be recruited on the basis of what they can offer in the future. For example, a nonprofit that is planning to purchase its first building would be well advised to seek finance committee members who are knowledgeable about the real-estate financing world. Larger institutions with complicated investments at the initial stages of an economic downturn might look for finance professionals with proven experience in conservative investment strategies, and so on.

It is good to remember that non–board member financial experts are also acceptable and useful candidates for the committee. A community leader or a business manager with suitable experience may be willing and interested in serving on the committee if he or she does not have to accept the rest of board responsibilities and liabilities.

3 The Audit Committee

In the previous chapter, we discussed the core responsibilities that all finance committees must fulfill. Now we will focus on the core duties that become evident when the complexity of the financial framework within an organization increases and the board decides that it is time to form a separate audit committee. Even if the finance committee has to perform double duty as the audit committee — as is done in most small- to medium-sized organizations — it is highly recommended that these two committees are separated and do not share members. This segregation of duties at the board level sets the primary example of how the organization takes independence of board members seriously and how it considers an independent audit as the ultimate form of oversight.

The following duties describe the functions of an audit committee.

Manage the Audit Relationship

The single most important financial relationship for any nonprofit is with the outside auditor(s). This also happens to be one of the most *misunderstood* relationships. Audit committee members should be very clear about what they can expect from their auditor, and vice versa.

Let's start with the auditor-board relationship. As the ultimate locus of responsibility in a nonprofit organization, the board — usually through its audit committee — must, in turn, hold the auditors accountable for producing the yearly audited financial statement. The auditor thus works for the full board of directors.

In practice, it often seems like the auditor reports to the financial staff. There are many reasons why this happens. The financial staff inevitably spends more face-to-face time with the auditor. Frequently, more turnover exists on the board of directors than in the finance staff or the audit staff, which means that the staff's relationship tends to be more consistent with the auditors. Often, the auditors and the financial staff are more likely to speak the same language and to be interested in the same professional matters than members of the board. Finally, in some cases, members of the financial staff may have once worked for the audit firm.

While such tendencies are understandable, they can also interfere with the audit committee's ability to both engage the outside auditor and manage the ongoing relationship. Happily, the audit committee can counteract the natural tendency for the financial staff to have a stronger relationship with the auditors. Most importantly, the full board of directors needs to insist on its primary role with the audit firm.

It is important to recognize that the yearly audit should be the beginning of a dialog, not the end of a process. The audit committee can arrange for regular meetings with the auditor throughout the year. Often, auditors are more than willing to meet regularly with audit committee members — and even the full board — but feel that the desire may not be mutual. It is to the advantage of your committee to encourage such ongoing meetings.

In most cases, an audit firm will issue a document called a *management letter* (see Appendix III for more information) at the end of each audit. This is a written document spelling out suggested improvements in the accounting system and certain financial management policies. The audit committee should receive a copy of this letter and be sure that the financial staff understands the recommendations and has a plan for carrying them out. (The accuracy and quality of the management letter is also, by implication, a way to gauge the quality of the audit firm itself.)

Audit committees should consider meeting with the audit firm in an executive session — without staff present. This gives the auditors an opportunity to be completely candid about the financial health of the organization, the adequacy of the financial systems, and the competence of the financial staff. While nonprofit staff members might understandably be anxious at the prospect of any board committee meeting without them, if the audit committee makes this a standard practice, it can help ease undue fear that financial personnel is being singled out for criticism. A further variation on this option is for the board to meet alone with the chief financial officer in order to encourage freer discussion than might occur with the chief executive present. These are powerful tools and should be used wisely and with forethought and planning.

Select the Independent Auditor

Since the board of directors is responsible for managing the audit relationship, it also has the duty of selecting the auditor. Again, this is an area where staff members are likely to have a great deal of influence in carrying out the actual tasks, but the audit committee needs explicitly to accept this oversight authority as part of its role.

Engaging an independent auditor is no different than contracting for any other professional service. It involves assessing the firm's (or individual CPA's) qualifications, capacity, and professional style. Members should plan to interview several candidates in person. References from comparable organizations are invaluable.

What should an auditor look like? What are some of the indicators that can help you find the most suitable and competent auditor for your organization? Start with professional credentials. Naturally, you want a certified public accountant who possesses the acumen needed for this job. Choose a professional or a firm that is familiar with the world of nonprofits and that hopefully has previously audited other nonprofits similar to yours. Make sure that the auditor understands the principal purpose for an audit: He or she is hired to assess and give an opinion on how accurately your financial statements reflect reality and that they are presented according to acceptable accounting principles. The auditor should also be able to provide you with helpful advice in the management letter that relates to your internal controls. And finally, you need an auditor who is not engaged in other procedures within the organization or who is providing any financial services that would make him or her audit personal activities.

Some nonprofits make the mistake of focusing primarily on the price in deciding whom to choose for an auditor. While understandable, this is short-term thinking. Auditors who carry out nonprofit audits are required to have a minimum amount of specialized continuing training in order to stay abreast of developments in the field. Indeed, many nonprofits' funding source requirements are so complex that the audit staff must have additional training or experience just to be able to audit them properly.

Auditors who focus on the nonprofit field are thus becoming increasingly specialized. Hiring an auditor on the basis of price alone may mean that the organization misses out on the kind of specialized sector knowledge that would help it function more effectively. It could be slow to adopt newly mandated regulations, and even miss critical developments altogether.

Ten Questions To Ask Your Auditor[1]

1. What internal controls are in place to prevent an employee, officer, or outside agent from intercepting checks intended for our organization prior to their being recorded in our books?
2. What controls are in place to prevent the unauthorized disbursement of funds from our bank accounts (general and payroll) by an employee or officer?
3. What controls are in place to prevent one of our vendors from overbilling our organization?
4. Are you aware of any forms of compensation or benefits received by our organization's officers, directors, or key employees that were not specifically approved by the board of directors?
5. Are you aware of any inappropriate or undisclosed relationships between officers, directors, key employees, vendors, or donors?
6. Are you aware of any relationships with vendors or contractors that appear to be less than ethical, warranting further inspection, or should otherwise be considered when putting out for competitive bid (e.g., relationships that have become too casual or close)?
7. Are there any individuals involved in the accounting process who wield excessive control or whose work is not subject to adequate review by another individual?
8. How would you characterize the morale, work environment, and professionalism of accounting personnel and senior management of our organization?
9. Overall, how would you rate our organization as to how well we are protected against fraud?
10. What is the most important step we could take to further protect our organization against fraud?

1. Zack, Gerard M. "Protect Your Organization against Fraud: Ten Questions You Should Ask Your Auditor" from *Board Member,* Vol. 7, Issue 4, April 1998. Washington, DC: BoardSource.

Manage the Scope of the Audit

Although staff routinely deals with the vast majority of day-to-day issues relating to the audit, the audit committee must be sure to understand, review, and approve the scope of the yearly audit. In doing so, it will find that the beginning and end of the yearly audit are simply milestones every year in the context of a sustained relationship and an ongoing process of oversight.

The audit committee should get a draft of the year's financial statements before they are issued, and meet with the auditors to be sure they understand the statements' meaning. Sometimes an auditor finds what are called *reportable conditions,* which are usually connected with the way government funds have been handled. Members need to be fully aware of any reportable conditions, and to make sure that staff members have followed up on them. Other details unrelated to government funding may surface during these discussions and need committee members' attention. Committee members also have the responsibility for dealing with personnel matters or serious breaches of internal controls that may be uncovered.

Besides ensuring that the external audit is carried out, the audit committee should consider requesting that occasional internal audits take place. An internal audit examines the financial structure, internal controls, risk management, processes and procedures, communication channels, policies, roles and duties of staff, explicit and implicit efficiencies and effectiveness of the systems, and so forth to assess the overall framework within which the organization is supposed to function and carry on business. This process unequivocally produces better results with the external audit.

Use the Independent Auditor as an Advisor

It may sound obvious, but one of the most productive things an audit committee can do is to listen to the independent auditor it hired. Every year the audit staff has a rare opportunity to spend some time inside the organization. Its members have an opportunity to look at just about anything they choose, examine operations and material in as much detail as they need, and rub elbows with the nonprofit's financial staff. The audit staff and the audit partner develop a wealth of information, formal and informal, about how the organization really runs. Why not tap into it?

Beyond the yearly conference, periodic telephone calls with quick questions are probably the most common and effective ways to use your organization's auditor. This practice is especially helpful when the organization faces new demands for the first time. It is also in the board's interest to work with the auditor before it makes any lasting financial decisions or commitments so that it can be assured of not making avoidable mistakes. At a minimum, the audit firm should keep the board updated on new regulations, reporting requirements, and government requirements.

Financial staff transitions are another way to use the auditor's knowledge and experience. When the chief financial staff person leaves, the auditor can often provide worthwhile guidance on what to look for in a replacement, as well as suggest any necessary reorganization of duties.

One thing the independent auditor should *not* do is to act in lieu of staff. Why not? Because auditors' independence is the most valuable asset they bring to their clients, even more than their knowledge. It is essential for everyone to understand that the auditor has no particular stake in how the organization operates. When an outside auditor also does routine accounting functions, such as monthly closings and other record-keeping tasks, there is reason to fear that their independence is impaired.

This practice of using the auditor to perform routine accounting work is at the heart of the auditor independence scandals that have beset the for-profit sector in the past few years. What makes this practice particularly troublesome for nonprofits is that it is surprisingly common in their world, especially in smaller or more rural organizations. The starkest example occurs when the auditor also does substantial work to keep the books up to date. This places the auditors in the position of auditing their own work — a clear-cut compromise of their independent status.

It can be hard to know when an auditor has crossed the line and has acquired a stake in how financial matters are decided. The accounting scandals and front page stories about corporate corruption mentioned above prompted changes in regulations and practices to ensure auditor independence, including measures governing when and how an audit firm can act as a consultant. It is prudent for the nonprofit audit committee to be conversant with those or any changing regulations even before the laws cover nonprofit organizations. Nothing replaces good practices and self-regulation.

Ensure Compliance with All Reporting Requirements

Audit reports of nonprofits are increasingly becoming more accessible to the public. Detailed financial information is within reach of anyone interested, because nonprofits are obligated to make their IRS Form 990s easily available as public documents. This availability puts greater pressure on nonprofits to make sure their publicly reported information is accurate.

The IRS Form 990 is considered an informational return, not a tax form. As a result, some nonprofit financial staff members, and even their auditors, take the form lightly. This is undesirable for several reasons. First, erroneous, inaccurate, or late informational returns can lead to complications — including severe excise taxes — should there ever be a question about other aspects of the nonprofit's situation. For the board, it is not enough to assume that the form has been filed. It should annually receive a copy with an indication of the timing of the filing.

More importantly, nonprofits are accountable to their stakeholders, including the taxpayers who indirectly subsidize them through their tax-exempt status. Sloppy or incorrect returns can erode a general sense of trust on the public's part. It is important to feel certain that your Form 990 is the best possible introduction to your organization — it looks professional and the attachments add to the presentation. Remember that donors and the media are paying more attention to public nonprofit financial reports, especially for elements like percentage of overhead charges and executives' salaries.

Funding sources, especially government agencies, often impose their own reporting requirements. These reports can also be informational in nature, but in a significant percentage of cases the quality and effectiveness of the reports can actually increase revenue or boost expenses. This increase is due to the fact that government funding comes with "strings" attached, demanding a more disciplined approach to accountability than is sometimes possible to achieve in an entirely privately funded environment.

For all of these reasons, audit committees need to be vigilant about making sure that their organization's reporting requirements have been met. External financial reporting is another one of those areas where staff will be far more involved than will the audit committee, but committee members should realize that they have a responsibility to see that the job gets done sufficiently.

4 The Investment Committee

Separate investment committees are created — and are actually necessary — only when an organization manages to accumulate sizable reserves, manages an important planned giving program, or has accumulated an endowment that needs special attention. It is unnecessary to have an investment committee if your major asset is your bank account. Until your board takes the step to creating a specific investment committee, the finance committee will most likely handle all investment-related issues.

Under most circumstances, it is not a wise idea to have your committee members undertake actual investment management tasks. Conflict-of-interest situations can influence unbiased decision making. The investment committee is an oversight committee that sets direction and guidelines for action. In this case, the committee's primary task would be to draft investment policies and ideally hire an independent professional investment manager who would report to the committee. Having committee members who understand the general investment framework — what constitutes risk, how to assess the risk your organization is ready to take; how the various investment vehicles relate to your accepted risk tolerance; and how the overall economic climate accommodates your fiscal needs — can only benefit your organization. The committee must also be able to translate the organization's sensitivity to social responsibility within the investment guidelines and avoid ethically or morally objectionable choices. As the supervisor of your investment manager, your committee is better equipped to monitor portfolio performance if its members have actual experience and knowledge about the realities that impact investment decisions.

As an oversight committee, the investment committee might work rather closely with a staff person whom management designates to handle the actual implementation of these policies. It is advisable to have the chief financial officer or the chief executive act as an ex officio (non–voting) member of the investment committee and in all committee meetings. He or she must ensure that staff members are present in meetings if they are responsible for implementing committee decisions.

Besides hiring a competent manager, the committee must draft policies that guide the manager in his or her decisions. These policies provide the committee with the parameters for evaluation. Besides defining the overall objectives of your investment approach and performance expectations, the policies guide the committee regarding any need for intervention. If long-term growth is more important than immediate return, the committee must learn patience. Reacting to every sudden market fluctuation is not wise financial oversight.

The following list constitutes the elements of an investment policy:

- Clarify your objectives relating to preservation and growth of the funds.
- Determine desirable asset mix to reflect your return expectations.
- Define acceptable asset quality for each portfolio category.
- Ensure adequate diversification to help avoid sudden major losses.
- Include guidelines for the manager's accountability and reporting requirements.
- Include an opinion or brief from an attorney on the Prudent Investor Rule (see Appendix II for a thorough definition).
- Define tolerance for loss when the principal of the investment is affected.
- Plan scenarios for handling unforeseen situations, such as substantial losses in main assets or overall financial stress within the organization requiring review of present investment objectives.

Service on an investment committee requires highly specialized skills. Committee members are charged to define the processes and procedures for safeguarding the organization's investment assets. This assumes a capacity to place the organization within a global market economy, provide a design for continuous and secure financial backing, evaluate ways to maximize returns and minimize losses, and manage to communicate the objectives and the results to the rest of the board.

5 Challenges of Combining Various Financial Committees

In the previous chapters we discussed the roles and duties of the main financial committees that a board may form. Creation of separate subcommittees often occurs in organizations that have multidisciplined or multitiered structures and relatively complicated financial systems, and with a board that is able to sustain different subgroups. Individuals involved in board member recruitment should include financially literate candidates in the candidate pool. The size of the board also allows the formation of committees or task forces without burdening individual board members with an unnecessarily heavy load of assignments.

The above, however, is more of an exception to the rule if we look at the entire nonprofit sector. Numerous nonprofits are modest grass-roots organizations with small, task-oriented boards and simple financial structures. Many nonprofits are in the between-phase — moving toward a more complicated and multifaceted financial structure but not yet able to diversify their boards. The full board may still act as a committee-of-the whole, or a single finance committee may be responsible for the entire aspect of fiscal oversight. This situation forces the board to accept new challenges and react to internal and external demands with heightened sensitivity.

The Combined Finance and Audit Committee

In today's environment of increased accountability, a finance committee that also is required to fulfill the duties of an audit committee is placed in a position of contradictions. Oversight of fiscal planning and operations, and ensuring independent audits and proper segregation of duties are directly linked but hierarchically unequal. Separating audit functions from all operational functions provides the premise for the most valued accountability the board can offer.

Committee members who serve in both capacities — audit and finance — must show exceptional diligence in their roles. The members must be able to separate the different hats they are wearing at different times. They must be cognizant of their operations oversight functions but able to shift gears when they get involved in communicating with the outside auditors. In reality, the auditors ultimately assess operations oversight as part of the full evaluation of an organization's financial management performance. An impartial committee member must learn to accept possible critique and implement suggested improvements.

In the next chapter, we will discuss in more detail how board independence no longer can be neglected or remain a negotiable issue.

The Executive Committee Absorbs the Finance Committee Tasks

The executive committee, which may act as a communication channel to the chief executive and usually has special authority to act on behalf of the full board between meetings or in urgent circumstances, occasionally is asked to take on the responsibilities of the finance committee as well. When this occurs, there is a subtle difference in managerial approach, which can potentially jeopardize the independent approach that remains so important to the culture of board financial oversight.

As we noted at the outset of this book, most nonprofit boards of directors, as a group, often do not feel like they have either the interest or the skill to carry out close oversight of the financial function. In effect, they erroneously "opt out" of the job and delegate it to a committee of the board such as the finance or finance-audit committee.

A consequence of that dynamic is that a good deal of financial oversight and even financial decision making gets transacted outside of the board's regular range of attention. A kind of "carve-out" effect can occur, in which the finance committee, financial staff, and auditors conduct their ongoing dialog with limited (if any) participation from members of the executive staff or nonfinancial members of the board. When this occurs, matters that are even vaguely financial in nature get shuffled off to the finance or audit committees, thus keeping the rest of the board even more isolated from the financial issues that impact the organization.

Auditors are expected to be independent of the groups they audit. In the same way, the financial staff needs to maintain an internally balanced role so as to be more credible when settling internal budget squabbles or conflicts over resources.

When the executive committee takes on the finance committee's role, these conflicting impulses between neutrality and active engagement can collide. In this collision, it is the audit focus that most often recedes. In effect, the finance-audit function becomes subordinate to the executive function. This diminishes the overall ability of the nonprofit to be accountable to its external stakeholders, because a key voice of independence is muted. While the situation in itself is certainly not fatal, it does make it harder for the organization to recognize and correct deficiencies in its financial management.

What's the answer? Once again, one solution in this case is to make sure that the board is aware of the difficulty of playing such different roles and keeps its dual responsibilities in mind. This requires education and constant self-reminders. It may also be possible to find one or more individuals for key executive committee roles whose personalities naturally incline toward the kind of independence typically exhibited by a good audit committee member. However, in general, combining the roles of the executive committee and the finance-audit committee undermines the tenets of segregation of duties.

When the Finance Committee Is Also the Fundraising Committee

The finance committee, on occasion, also assumes responsibility for fundraising. The intent here is to create a single committee that should be responsible for all facets of money management. This, however, is a problematic combination of duties. The demands of the finance committee and those of fundraising are quite different, with the tendency to attract very different types of personalities and skills in those wanting to be involved. It is close to impossible to reconcile these differences. Members of a finance committee need expertise and understanding of financial planning and management, whereas fundraising primarily relies on people skills, the ability to communicate to funders the special role the organization plays in alleviating social malfunctions, or providing educational or cultural rewards to its constituents.

If, however, it is necessary to combine these two functions, the resolution of the contradiction often occurs in a natural sort of way, as certain individuals will tend to gravitate to one function or the other. In effect, the larger committee may bifurcate into two distinct subcommittees of the larger committee that simply coordinates their work.

A slightly more common variation on this theme is for the finance committee to oversee management of the endowment. Large donations should ordinarily be professionally managed. When the gift is substantive but not large enough to justify professional management, however, the finance committee might take on the job. Here too, individuals are likely to self-identify themselves with one distinct set of responsibilities or another. Some members focus on raising additional funds for the endowment; others concentrate on fund management.

6 The Finance Committee's Role in Maintaining Independence

Nonprofits are expected by their nature to adhere to a higher standard of moral and ethical behavior than just about any other part of our society, except perhaps for government. This is part of the implicit exchange that makes nonprofit public charities (also known as 501(c)(3) corporations) tax exempt, which allows them to grant a tax deduction to donors. A central tenet of this higher standard is that all parties concerned must be independent of any undue external influence to act in their own self-interest. The finance committee has a responsibility to see that all parties adhere to these standards and act independently at all times on behalf of the nonprofit's best interest.

There are really two key groups who must maintain a proper independence with respect to their involvement in the nonprofit: the directors and officers, and the auditors. Each has the same responsibility but must go about it in different ways. We will address each group's task of maintaining independence separately.

Directors' and Officers' Independence

For our purposes, directors and officers will be considered the members of the board and those on staff who control transactions with outsiders. Typically, included among staff insiders will be the chief executive, the chief financial officer, and other senior managers who can routinely enter transactions on behalf of the organization.

The analogy with insider trading on Wall Street is instructive here. An example of illegal insider stock transactions are those in which company insiders sell their shares of the company upon learning bad news that has not been released to the public. The rough equivalents in the nonprofit world are called *excess benefit transactions* and *related-party transactions*. These occur, for instance, when a nonprofit insider engages in a transaction that favors — or appears to favor — the interests of the insider at the expense of the nonprofit, with the benefit to the insider exceeding the value of the service rendered.

In a hypothetical example, a board chair who signs a lease on behalf of the nonprofit for a building that she and her husband own is engaging in a related-party transaction. She is on both sides of the transaction, helping make a decision where she is also at the receiving end. In the actual consequences of the transaction, whether it is a good deal for the organization or a bad deal doesn't matter; it is still a related-party transaction.

Here is the twist that brings the judgment of the board and the finance committee into play: Very few economic transactions not involving national security are illegal in American society. The board chair example noted on the previous page is not a prohibited transaction — except in the case of a private foundation. But if not illegal, might it be unethical? Or, on the other hand, might it be a legitimate opportunity, which the nonprofit is well advised to shrewdly seize? One needs to know the facts of each case in order to answer those questions. It is up to the finance or audit committee to take the lead in ensuring such relevant facts are available.

The first and best line of defense for a nonprofit in which a related-party transaction occurs is disclosure of the facts. This is why related-party transactions will usually be disclosed in the footnotes of the audited financial statement. If a transaction is not illegal or otherwise prohibited, so the reasoning goes, then let it be publicly known so that outsiders can make their own determination.

The best policy is to remain proactive. The finance or audit committee should take responsibility for seeing that the board has written policies and procedures in place for defining and dealing with related-party transactions before they occur. To ensure compliance — and to remind members of the policies — the committee should require each individual board member and corporate officer to sign a statement of independence each year. When related-party transactions are unavoidable, the board should follow a proscribed course of action, such as a thorough discussion of the possible transaction and its implications, and recusal of the involved board member from all votes. It is not necessarily the impaired independence itself that damages the nonprofit as it is the appearance of secrecy and unacknowledged double dealing.

Auditor Independence

In recent years, there has been a significant change in the ways that outside auditors define independence and in how they act upon that definition. As noted earlier, this issue was catalyzed for the public by corporate accounting scandals.

The two latest developments are the General Accounting Office's (GAO) amendment to its *Government Auditing Standards*, and the Sarbanes-Oxley Act (please refer to Appendix II for concise definitions). Of the two, the GAO regulation is the most directly relevant to nonprofits. GAO regulations affect organizations that receive government funding or contracts and therefore must draft reports and set in place procedures that meet government codes. However, the Sarbanes-Oxley Act, which deals mainly with publicly held companies, will almost certainly have a profound indirect impact on perceptions about auditors and audit committees in the nonprofit world as well. Several state attorneys general are closely following the impact of the Sarbanes-Oxley Act on public corporations and may consider implementing similar laws for nonprofits under their sphere of control.

GAO Independence Standards

Since 1972, the General Accounting Office has drafted standards covering audit processes for those nonprofits that receive government funding. The most significant recent changes in the GAO's standards, issued in January 2002, deal with non–audit, or consulting services. Although it applies principally to those nonprofit entities receiving more than $500,000 in federal funds, the new regulation can be expected to influence the sector in general if its provisions become accepted as a model for how to purchase auditing and consulting services in the future.

The GAO standards reflect a relatively new way of setting auditing standards in that they are deliberately based on principles rather than rules. This is seen as a way to more fully cover scenarios that might not be explicitly prohibited by a rule but which virtually any reasonable person would recognize as questionable. For example, the independence standard reads as follows:

"In all matters relating to the audit work, the audit organization and the individual auditor, whether government or public, should be free both in fact and in appearance from personal, external, and organizational impairments to independence."

Note that this formulation sets general yet actionable parameters without being overly specific in what it allows or prohibits. The regulation goes on to say that the independence standards are based on two overarching principles:

1. Auditors should not perform management functions or make management decisions.
2. Auditors should not audit their own work or provide non–audit services in situations where the amounts or services involved are significant or material to the subject matter of the audit.

Audit services that do not violate these standards must meet additional tests. Individuals performing the non–audit services should not work on the related audit; an audit organization's work must not be artificially reduced; services must be documented and must meet certain quality assurance safeguards.

Many audit organizations have followed these standards, or something very similar, for years. But some have not. The problem of auditor independence is particularly acute in rural areas with few financial advisors, and with small or unsophisticated nonprofits. Finance committees of nonprofits subject to the GAO standards should be aware of the possibility of violating them given the current legal context.

A nonprofit receiving any public funding must be ready to be subjected to a battery of requirements that sometimes may even turn the money into a burden rather than a blessing. Government and state agencies that contract with or simply provide straightforward financial assistance to nonprofits usually — above and beyond the above standards — require conscientious reporting from the recipient. These demands can be so extensive that they may create a domino effect and force the organization to assess and readjust many of its existing processes and capacities. To be able to respond to the government agency's demands, the organization may have to redesign its accounting processes to produce the necessary reports, start keeping different data that it needed before, disclose information that was not available to outsiders previously, increase its technological capacity to accommodate a complicated report function, and hire additional staff to report to funders and keep them informed.

Sarbanes-Oxley Act

July 2002 was an important time in the life of American publicly traded companies. A new law became effective to help eliminate the wave of disastrous financial scandals that kept ruining some major companies. Shareholders trust had been shaken and stricter laws were expected to restore that faith. The Sarbanes-Oxley Act set new rules and regulations to guide auditors of public companies and the audit committees of these corporations' boards.

The nonprofit sector may be influenced by the repercussions of this new law if similar provisions are adopted to govern nonprofit corporations. It makes sense for individual organizations to be proactive, study the clauses, and independently determine which issues provide a solid and sensible framework for their own operations.

Here are some key provisions of the law:

- Each board must have an audit committee with independent members. This is to ensure that management is separated from auditing its own work.
- Certain non–audit consulting services are prohibited from being performed for a client by their audit firm. This ensures that auditors do not audit their own activities.
- Partners must rotate off an engagement after five years. Rotating chief auditors provides an added layer of independence and new eyes looking at the records of the organization.
- Audit committees must disclose the name of at least one "financial expert" member. It is important to have competent and financially literate members of the committee who must communicate with the auditor and interpret the audit report.
- Most personal loans to a company's executives are prohibited.
- The auditor must report on the company's internal controls. Each corporation must have written policies on internal controls, which is understood to be a public document.
- Company executives must vouch for certain reports and controls. Chief executives and chief financial officers must certify the financial statements to testify their accuracy.

Board member independence does not relate to only excluding staff from serving on the board and its financial committees. Independence above all refers to objectivity, unbiased decision making, lack of conflict of interest, and separating personal benefit from organizational priorities. Auditor independence brings the desired seal of integrity one step closer.

Conclusion

The financial committee of a nonprofit organization is truly at the heart of the public's trust. Members of this group are asked to do a task with which many of their colleagues are unfamiliar and uncomfortable. There is no standard model for committees of this type, but because of the full board's ultimate responsibility and fiduciary obligation to its organization, it holds the authority to delegate various tasks to a single financial committee or multiple committees. This chosen structure depends on several factors, including organizational size, complexity of financial activities, multiple sources of funding and revenue streams, and regulatory oversight. The stronger these factors, the stronger the rationale for creating separate financial committees. Boards that are able to separate financial tasks among individual committees are usually better positioned to ensure a full focus on key duties for each.

To make the duties of financial committees easier to understand, we have categorized and addressed them in the text as core duties versus non–core duties. Core duties can be considered the minimum responsibilities likely to be assigned to a finance committee, while non–core duties are those functions that are likely to be assigned to other committees, subcommittees, or tasks forces in larger, more complex organizations.

It is the primary responsibility of the finance committee to act as the internal watchdog of independence in any nonprofit organization. By sustaining the collective group of fiscal committees and their individual tasks, overseeing financial planning of the organization, and ensuring the proper education and reporting of the board, an organization's finance committee can concentrate on general fiscal oversight, while other financial groups of the board tackle more focused issues.

It has always been critical for the audit committee, specifically, to understand fully its responsibilities. But in recent years the audit committee has received heightened attention in all sectors of the American economy. To help justify the public trust, board members as well as staff must be independent of questionable business dealings with their organization, and the organization's auditing firm must be equally independent of potential and real conflicts of interest. It is in this latter area that recent laws and regulations underscore the need for independence. Consequently, the pressure on this group is greater than it has ever been.

When and if an organization has accumulated significant reserves or an endowment, it begins to look to the establishment of a separate investment committee. This committee acts in the capacity of an oversight committee that sets the direction and parameters for investment of the organization's assets, and not the actual management. The committee creates and develops investment policies, which will guide those tasked with managing the assets.

In today's vision, nonprofits are held to a higher standard of behavior than any entity in the private sector. Many in the nonprofit world take this standard of conduct for granted, not realizing that it could be compromised by unintended lapses in attention or policies. It takes dedication and effectiveness to make sure that the nonprofit's assets, including its reputation, are properly safeguarded. The skill and knowledge of financial committee members are critical to making that happen.

Appendix I

Summary of Core and Non–Core Duties of Financial Committees

Core Duties: **The Finance Committee**	*Non–Core Duties:* **When the Finance Committee is also the Audit Committee**	*Non–Core Duties:* **When the Finance Committee is also the Investment Committee**
Oversee organizational financial planning.	Hire independent auditor.	Draft investment policies for the organization.
Safeguard organizational assets.	Review the audit report with the auditor.	Hire and oversee performance of a professional investment manager.
Draft organizational fiscal policies.	Ensure that appropriate internal controls are in place.	Set performance goals for the portfolio.
Monitor that adequate funds are available for the plan.	Request internal audit from time to time.	Follow closely the markets and their development.
Anticipate financial problems.	Help board adopt a conflict-of-interest policy.	Follow new regulations and judicial interpretation of investment-related rules.
Ensure that accurate and complete records are kept.	Assure the board that the financial statements reflect the organization's financial condition.	Plan scenarios for unforeseen situations affecting invested assets.
See that the board receives accurate and timely reports and help other board members understand financial statements as well as the general financial situation of the organization.	See that all laws and regulations are respected.	Consider all morally responsible investment concerns.
Make sure that federal, state, and local reporting takes place.	See that all affairs in the organization are conducted ethically.	Report to the rest of the board.

Appendix II

Useful Terms

The following regulators or regulations influence the financial and auditing activities of nonprofits. Be aware of their roles and become familiar with their authority related to your organization.

AICPA — American Institute of Certified Public Accountants
AICPA is the professional organization for CPAs. All members must meet specific standards and follow rules set by this organization relating to accounting procedures.

FASB — Financial Accounting Standards Board
Since 1973, FASB has been the designated organization for establishing standards of financial accounting and reporting. Those standards (GAAP) govern the preparation of financial reports.

GAAP — Generally Accepted Accounting Principles
These principles set and guide your minimum standard accounting procedures and clarify the appropriate format and structure of your financial statements. Regular changes are adopted in response to the recommendations and new rules adopted by FASB and AICPA.

GAAS — Generally Accepted Auditing Standards
Auditors must follow these rules in their line of work. These standards address quality control, professional care, and independence of auditors.

GAO — General Accounting Office
This investigative arm of Congress sets general accounting standards for nonprofits that receive federal funds ("Yellow Book").

Prudent Investor Rule
The Prudent Investor Rule is a legal doctrine, which provides guidance to investment managers regarding the standards for managing an investment portfolio in a legally satisfactory manner. This rule is comprised of both the UPIA and the UMIFA.

Sarbanes-Oxley Act
The American Competitiveness and Corporate Accountability Act of 2002, commonly known as the Sarbanes-Oxley Act, was enacted in July 2002 mainly to regulate the audits and audit committees of publicly traded companies (two clauses cover all organizations: the whistle-blower clause and the regulations on document destruction). The impact of this law may affect the auditing practices of individual nonprofit organizations as well.

UMIFA — Uniform Management of Institutional Funds Act
UMIFA, adopted by most states, governs endowment spending by nonprofit corporations and some trusts. It allows grantmaking based on interest, dividends, *and* realized and unrealized capital gains. To invest in this manner, state laws usually require that UMIFA be adopted by resolution. This act also instituted a spending floor — a fund's historic dollar value. The law does not allow grants from funds below that value, which protects permanent funds from being entirely eroded.

UPIA — Uniform Prudent Investor Act
Completed by the Uniform Law Commissioners in 1994, this act removes much of the common law restriction upon the investment authority of trustees of trusts and like fiduciaries. It allows such fiduciaries to employ modern portfolio theory to guide investment decisions. Performance is measured on the total return of the whole portfolio, not upon the performance of each investment separately. The act allows the fiduciary to delegate investment decisions to qualified and supervised agents and requires sophisticated risk-return analysis to guide investment decisions.

Appendix III

The Management Letter

By the time auditors finish their work each year, they have gathered a great deal of information about their client. Much of this information goes into the audited financial statements. But some of the findings and conclusions essential for the nonprofit board to understand are not necessarily appropriate for public disclosure. The *management letter* provides a handy way of communicating this kind of helpful information, which might otherwise get lost.

What Goes into the Management Letter?

Unlike the audited financial statements, management letters are not governed by detailed rules regarding what is included and how it is displayed. In fact, most of what is in the management letter is a matter of the audit firm's judgment.

Often, the management letter discusses matters related to the accounting system. These will be observations about practices the audit staff made as they carried out the research and testing for the audit. They may also include observations about policies and procedures that need improvement.

The technical content of this material is well suited to the nonprofit's accounting staff, since the auditors are similarly trained and comfortable with the terminology. There may also be aspects of the management letter that go beyond accounting to higher level commentary about financial strategy or overall financial health, which senior executives and board members will find useful.

Two relatively recent trends, however, work against auditors who choose to include those types of higher-level comments. First, the rapid adoption of computers and the hiring of better trained nonprofit accounting staff have rendered many of the kind of findings that auditors had often included in their management letters in the past unnecessary. This dynamic has undercut much of the conventional content of management letters, shrinking the available technical recommendations that auditors can make.

Second, in some areas government funders — aware of the existence of management letters — are beginning to request copies of them. Auditors' management letter comments could easily be construed as a criticism of their clients, so the possibility of government funders reading the management letter seems to have had somewhat of a chilling effect on their usefulness. Auditors faced with the possibility of embarrassing a client in writing are motivated to look for other ways to communicate suggestions for improvement.

SUGGESTED RESOURCES

Accountability: The Buck Stops Here. Special Edition of *Board Member*. BoardSource, 2002. From financial statements to mission statements, ultimate accountability lies in the board's hands. And, as the public endures a seemingly unending string of accountability scandals in the for-profit sector, nonprofits realize that embracing their responsibilities is as crucial as ever. This issue explores the many facets of accountability and examines the lessons nonprofits can learn from the crisis in the corporate world.

Axelrod, Nancy R. *Advisory Councils*. Washington, DC: BoardSource, 2004. This book expands the traditional way of looking at the concept of advisory councils, exploring ways in which they can help the board to keep its own magnitude in check without losing impact. Nancy Axelrod proves that these groups have more functions than usually assigned, and explains the role an advisory council can play in helping your board to expand outreach efforts, find new supporters, incorporate new perspectives, and distribute tasks.

Berger, Steven. *Understanding Nonprofit Financial Statements*. Washington, DC: BoardSource, 2003. The newly revised and expanded edition of this best-selling title includes key accounting terms and concepts, important benchmarking ratios, and sample nonprofit financial statements. Steven Berger's no-nonsense explanations are helpful for board members, treasurers, finance committee members, and staff who prepare financial information for the board.

Bobowick, Marla J., Sandra R. Hughes and Berit M. Lakey. *Transforming Board Structure: Strategies for Committees and Task Forces*. Washington, DC: BoardSource, 2001. This book provides a fresh look at committees and how your board can use work groups to streamline the work of the full board. Discover the importance of reducing the number of standing committees and relying more on ad hoc groups and task forces.

Dietel, William M. and Linda R. Dietel. *The Board Chair Handbook*. Washington, DC: BoardSource, 2001. This handbook includes a complete guide to the chair's roles and responsibilities, suggestions for developing board policies and procedures, recommendations for handling a variety of problems, and advice for cultivating talent for future board leadership. Also included is a diskette containing sample meeting agendas and customizable letters for asking a board member for a gift, cultivating and recruiting prospective board members, inviting someone to join the board, and more.

Fry, Robert P. *Creating and Using Investment Policies: A Guide for Nonprofit Boards*. Washington, DC: BoardSource, 1997. As the financial conditions of a nonprofit improve and a reserve fund becomes a reality, the board members have the difficult task of deciding how to best manage and invest the funds. This book answers many of the questions concerning the basics of investing, the legal basis for investment theory, cash management issues, necessity for an investment advisor, and the appropriate board member involvement in investment management.

Greenfield, James M. *Fundraising Responsibilities of Nonprofit Boards*. Washington, DC: BoardSource, 2003. Discover why fundraising is important and why board members should be involved. Included are practical suggestions for board members in direction, planning, and oversight of fundraising. Help your board succeed in the three phases of fundraising — cultivation, solicitation, and stewardship.

Lakey, Berit M., Sandra R. Hughes and Outi Flynn. *Governance Committee*. Washington, DC: BoardSource, 2004. Governance committees are essential in every board because of their ability to ensure full board effectiveness. This book illustrates how a governance committee not only recruits new members, but also transforms those recruits into productive and capable board members. The authors outline duties of the governance committee and provide helpful hints and guidelines on who should serve on this committee, how to determine what kinds of members your board needs, where to find these individuals, and how to orient and continuously educate your board.

Lang, Andrew S. *Financial Responsibilities of Nonprofit Boards*. Washington, DC: BoardSource, 2003. Provide your board members with an understanding of their financial responsibilities including an overview of financial oversight and ways to ensure against risk. Written in non-technical language, this book will help your board understand financial planning, the IRS Form 990, and the audit process. Also included are financial board and staff job descriptions and charts on all the financial documents and reports, including due dates and filing procedures.

Light, Mark. *Executive Committee*. Washington, DC: BoardSource, 2004. Executive committees are known to take on too much power, often resulting in confusion among the rest of the board members. Find out in which situations executive committees may be beneficial, and in what circumstances they may not be imperative. Also included in this book is a description of who should serve on this committee and the intent of the committee's relationship with the board.

McLaughlin, Thomas A. *Presenting: Nonprofit Financials*. Washington, DC: BoardSource, 2001. *Presenting: Nonprofit Financials* is a ready-made on-screen presentation that can be used as a traditional graphics presentation, as overhead transparency slides, or printed out for handouts. Each slide is accompanied by a set of presentation notes and talking points to guide the discussion. Also included is a 12-page user's guide with suggestions for training board members on their financial responsibilities, instructions for using the presentation, and tips for providing proper fiduciary oversight.

Sorrells, Michael and Andrew S. Lang. *The IRS Form 990: A Window into Nonprofits*. Washington, DC: BoardSource, 2001. This book describes the Form 990 and its purposes, and includes a step-by-step guide through each part of the form. Also included is a discussion of the filing requirements and disclosure rules. The authors point to sensitive areas that the board should pay particular attention to before submitting.

Tempel, Eugene R. *Development Committee*. Washington, DC: BoardSource, 2004. Motivating board members to be actively involved in fundraising is one of the greatest challenges nonprofit charities face; learn how a development committee can help with this challenge. This book clarifies the role of development committees, outlining how they can help with fundraising goals by serving as the board's internal fundraising trainer, motivator, and overseer, and including a discussion on the committee's relationship with development staff and an introduction to the use of organizational development committees.

About the Author

Thomas A. McLaughlin currently serves as Senior Manager of Not-for Profit Management Consulting at Grant Thornton LLP, and has over 25 years of nonprofit experience as a nonprofit manager, trade association executive, and management consultant. Mr. McLaughlin joined Grant Thornton in 2001, following 11 years as Practice Leader for the Nonprofit Management Consulting practice at BDO Seidman, LLP. At Grant Thornton, he assists all types of nonprofit clients with strategic, operations, and financial projects. Mr. McLaughlin is nationally recognized as an expert in nonprofit mergers and alliances, financial management, and strategic planning.

Among his previous positions, Mr. McLaughlin served as an executive with two major Massachusetts social service agencies and as Associate Director of the Massachusetts Council of Human Service Providers. He is currently on the management faculty at Brandeis University and Boston University, where he teaches MBA and MSW graduate students. Mr. McLaughlin was the first Nonprofit Scholar in Residence at the Isenberg School of Management at the University of Massachusetts/ Amherst. He also serves on the Board of Directors of the Massachusetts Council of Human Service Providers and has previously served on the board of directors of both the Make-a-Wish Foundation of Greater Boston and Family Service, Inc.

Mr. McLaughlin earned a Bachelor of Arts degree, a Master of Urban Affairs degree, and a Master of Business Administration degree from Boston University. He is the author of four publications, was previously a columnist for the *Boston Business Journal*, and is currently a contributing editor and columnist for the *Nonprofit Times*.

About the Firm

Grant Thornton is the leading global accounting, tax, and business advisory firm dedicated to serving the needs of middle-market companies and not-for-profit organizations. Founded in 1924, Grant Thornton serves middle-market and not-for-profit clients through 51 offices in the United States, and in more than 650 offices in 109 countries through Grant Thornton International.

Grant Thornton's Web site address is www.GrantThornton.com.